INSIDE THE REVOLVING DOOR: CHRONICLES FROM THE HUMAN RESOURCES DEPARTMENT

xoxox

Vana M. Session

Foreword by Dana Dane

DEDICATION

Dedicated to my fellow Human Resources (HR) colleagues, who know the struggle we face every day inside the revolving doors of organizations across the world.

Thank you to my husband, for always supporting my crazy ideas. I get bored easily! Thank you to my son...just for being YOU, and being my personal "HR challenge."

TABLE OF CONTENTS

FOREWORD

When I think about excellence, I think about people who have overcome their circumstances to become recognized as exceptional in their field, endeavors or goals. Names like Oprah, Serena, Jordan and Ali come to mind… and now Tana.

I have had the pleasure and honor of watching my wife, Tana, set goals and exceed those goals. Her drive and ambition are inspiring. She has never been satisfied with mediocre and continues to leap out of her comfort zone so she can reach new heights and achievements. Her determination to be better…to be stellar…to be great…are only trumped by her love of God and her family.

As her husband, I am proud of her past and extremely excited to be a part of her future endeavors. This is just the beginning of a new chapter in her life! Bravo! Congratulations! Continued greatness!

All my love.
Dana Dane

CHAPTER 1
FROM LONDON TO
NEW YORK TO HONG KONG

Kevin was a rainmaker who worked for an international hedge fund. The company had locations in London, New York and Hong Kong. Kevin was an Italian gentleman, tall and handsome with dark hair and ocean-blue eyes. He was very charismatic and personable.

Throughout his career, Kevin established an astounding reputation with clients in London. He was able to go in and close a deal like none other! If someone had problems closing a deal, they would call Kevin and he would go in and charm the client and seal the deal. This was his talent! He also established himself as the office flirt. Kevin was married with two kids...but that did not stop him from hitting on other women, in particular, the new young interns who joined the company every summer. He also had a thing for the clients who he deemed to be attractive. He definitely had a "type": tall, slim and blonde.

Kevin experienced many complaints from female employees over a two-year period in the London office. After managing complaints as discreetly as possible, it became apparent to the local HR Director and leadership team that a sexual-harassment lawsuit or a class action lawsuit would be filed against him sooner or later. Fortunately, before this happened the company was able to secure a new client — a big client — in New York. It was the perfect opportunity to transfer him out of the London office before the inevitable happened.

The way the leadership team sold the idea of relocating to Kevin was by explaining to him they needed him in New York to manage a particularly difficult client. They emphasized he was the only one who could handle the client, as they feared losing the deal, which was a multi-million-dollar investment opportunity.

Kevin was open to the idea and accepted the offer. Kevin decided to relocate to New York first, then his wife and children would join him in the summer to avoid disrupting their school year.

The HR Director in New York collaborated with the HR Director in London and conducted confidential, off the record, conversations about Kevin. The London HR Director informed the New York HR Director of the various complaints and issues Kevin had with young ladies, in particular, when he would go to happy-hour events after work. The London HR Director confidentially shared with her New York colleague part of the reason for this immediate transfer was the local London leadership's fear that, eventually, someone would file a harassment complaint. But because he was a rainmaker, and everyone in the company knew he was a rainmaker, "mum was the word" regarding his behavior. No one complained and no one said anything, because they knew they would probably lose THEIR job before Kevin would lose his.

The New York HR Director met with the New York CEO and shared the information with him. The CEO told the HR Director not to worry about it. He assured the HR Director Kevin had been "spoken to," and he was aware of what their expectations were of him when he arrived in New York. He was to behave himself and "keep it in his pants!" The HR Director decided to just manage it and hoped they would not have any issues with him since he had already been advised by both CEOs — the one in London and the one in New York.

Fast-forward to three months later, Kevin was working in New York attending to the client, making good relationships and securing additional investments with other clients. Everything was running smoothly. Summer recruiting was in full swing. HR had to recruit summer interns to work for Kevin's client as well as new graduates fresh out of college. Kevin insisted on being on the interview panels so he could make certain the "right" people with the right personalities were being selected for his clients. He, of course, favored all of the female candidates. At first, no one really noticed his pattern, until they really started paying attention to who Kevin wanted to hire: all women and all blonde. For the HR Director, this was a red flag and he immediately insisted on more diversity in the selection process. The HR Director sat on the next interview panel instead of just letting the recruiters handle it, so he could have some influence over who was being recruited. Due to the HR Director's efforts, they were able to diversify the candidate pool and, ultimately, whom they extended offers to for their various open positions.

One of the recent new hires was a senior-level sales executive (female and blonde) who was assigned to one of Kevin's key clients. Since she was a senior sales executive, she had to spend a lot of time with Kevin and the client, which involved dinners, cocktail hours, etc. It also involved traveling, because the client had locations in different cities.

On a particular trip to Boston, the sales executive actually complained to the HR Director that she felt Kevin was coming on to her, and he was being inappropriate in the way he touched her. She insisted it was unwarranted and unwanted. After all, she was married with kids as well.

The sales executive was aware Kevin was married and that his family had not relocated to the States yet. Kevin openly shared information about he and his wife having an open marriage. The sales executive felt very uncomfortable hearing this, and she wanted her concerns on record. She reiterated to the HR Director she was NOT interested in pursuing a personal relationship with Kevin. She also informed the HR Director she would refuse to travel with Kevin or do any additional dinners with him and clients if his inappropriate behavior continued.

The HR Director informed the CEO, who insisted the sales executive needed to "go with the flow" since Kevin was a key rainmaker for the organization. He also confirmed the sales executive would go before Kevin would, if it ever came down to who would lose their job. The HR Director did not share this information with the sales executive, but he decided to keep his eye on Kevin, and just really keep up with what was happening with him when he was at the client dinners and cocktail hours. The HR Director started making direct observations of his own, and noticed some of Kevin's behaviors were inappropriate. Kevin was prone to making very rude and crass jokes, which oftentimes were of a sexual nature. On more than one occasion the HR Director witnessed Kevin mentioning he had an open marriage to the young female staff.

The HR Director waited two days and called Kevin into his office. When he confronted Kevin about his behavior, Kevin made a joke of it and said he did not mean anything by it. Plus…no one was taking him up on his offer anyway! Really?! He went on to say how people in the U.S. were stuck-up prudes, and they just did not understand the European sense of humor. This really made the HR Director second-guess himself. Maybe it was not as bad as he had originally thought? Maybe it was not as bad as the sales executive perceived? Maybe it was just a true lack of understanding of the culture or the sense of humor coming from abroad. On that note, the HR Director dismissed his concerns and reservations.

Shortly thereafter, Kevin sent an email to someone named "Rachel", and assumed it was one of the new hires who started with the company that summer. Instead, he erroneously sent it to the client, whose name was also Rachel. As a result, the client contacted the HR Director and the CEO, and shared Kevin's email with them. In his email, Kevin described what it would be like to sleep with him and how it would be "life-changing," and she needed to experience a "real man" instead of college boys or "lads," as he referred to them in the email.

The HR Director and the CEO decided they needed to have another talk with Kevin, which they did together. They also hired an external consultant to come in and teach him about U.S. sexual-harassment laws in the workplace. His previous training was in London, and he had not completed the online U.S. training required of him when he transferred. Supposedly, he skipped the training because he was too busy traveling and meeting with his new clients. Kevin stated the training was not at the top of his list of priorities.

The external consultant was hired to work with Kevin for approximately 60 days. He had to meet with her once a week for 1½ hours. The consultant presented different scenarios to him, asking if he saw how certain behaviors would be considered inappropriate. She also presented him with his email and asked him to explain what he was trying to achieve when he sent it. In his response, he appeared to be embarrassed about the situation and even came across as very humble and meek.

The consultant presented her final assessment to the CEO and the HR Director. In the report, she stated the following: 1) she did not think that he took the process seriously; 2) she felt Kevin was trying to use psychology on her; and 3) he tried to use his charm on her, flashing his blue eyes, handsome looks and Italian accent. From meeting with him, she could see how it could be easy for women, especially young, impressionable women, to be flattered by his attention. Her recommendation was that he not work for the company anymore because he was a huge liability. It just so happened he did become a liability, as the sales executive did NOT go away.

About a month later, Kevin and the sales executive were scheduled to be on a business trip to Florida. The meeting was an early morning one, so the sales executive decided to arrive a day early. Since she had a day off, she wanted to make use of the hotel pool. After going for a swim, she laid out and enjoyed the Florida sunshine, since the weather was much more inviting than in New York. Kevin spotted her poolside as he, too, had arrived a day early. He was not aware he and the sales executive were arriving on the same day, as she had been avoiding him unless absolutely necessary.

In an investigative interview held later with the HR Director and the CEO, Kevin reported he only went to the pool area to sit at the bar since his room was not ready. He went on to say he just happened to look around the pool area, only to find the sales executive lying poolside. His next move was where things took a turn for the worse.

Kevin walked over to her lounge chair and straddle her, lying chest to chest with her. This scared the sales executive, as she was dozing off and, with her shades on, she was unaware anyone was approaching. She pushed him and immediately jumped off the chair because she assumed she was under attack. Once she got her bearings, she grabbed her towel and went to her room crying hysterically. She contacted the HR Director on his cell phone and explained to him what had just happened. She was in no shape to meet with the client, so she decided to fly back to New York on the first available flight that day. She let the HR Director know she would be in his office first thing in the morning. When Monday morning rolled around, the sales executive was in the HR Director's office filing a sexual-harassment claim against Kevin. Oy vey!

After a full investigation, it was determined the company would offer the sales executive compensation to make her "go away." Initially, she declined their offer but, in the end, she walked away with almost $500,000, a clean record and a favorable recommendation from the CEO. She has since moved on to a new company and is happy at this stage of her life.

About six months later, Kevin was transferred to Hong Kong, where he is currently working. The employment rules were just as strict, if not more so, in Hong Kong. But it just so happened the new client he was assigned to had very few female staff members, and the local HR team were made aware of the issues with Kevin. They were very keen about what types of females they aligned with the client to ensure they were not Kevin's "type" at all. So far, there have been no complaints of any type of inappropriate behavior from Kevin. His wife and kids eventually joined him in Hong Kong. In the end, Kevin joked that he was in corporate exile. Oh, well!!

CHAPTER 2

SHE DRANK HER WAY OUT OF A JOB

An HR Director received a call from her call center Supervisor who shared employees were complaining about one of their co-workers, Sheila, who smelled like alcohol whenever she returned from the bathroom. The Supervisor found this difficult to believe because Sheila was the epitome of a high performer (HiPo) and one of her favorite staff members. She would extend herself to help train new staff members; organize team birthday parties; and went out of her way to go above and beyond her required duties. Sheila was also a stellar call center employee, as she always surpassed the approved hold time as well as the time to resolve callers' issues. She always received high reviews and was recognized multiple times as *Employee of the Month*.

The Supervisor wanted to find out from Human Resources what, if anything, she could do if the reports were true.

The HR Director instructed the Supervisor to first have a conversation with Sheila. If the Supervisor truly suspected she was drinking on the job, she should report to Human Resources along with the employee to have a confidential meeting.

The next day, the Supervisor followed the advice of the HR Director and had a conversation with Sheila. As they spoke, the HR Director detected the smell of alcohol on Sheila's breath. She asked Sheila if she had been drinking, and her response was, "No, I don't drink…I don't do alcohol! It's probably my mouthwash that you're smelling because I use Listerine." The Supervisor viewed this as plausible, so she dismissed her concerns.

A few days later, when Sheila pulled open her desk drawer, an employee who was sitting right next to her just happened to look down and saw what she thought was a can of beer. She immediately went to the Supervisor and said, "I know you spoke to Sheila, and I don't know what the two of you spoke about, but I think I see a can of beer in her desk drawer." Keep in mind this is a call center, so all of the employees have open desks. Employees sit very close to one another, there is very little privacy, they can hear each other's conversations, and even see what their neighbor eats and drinks at their desks throughout the day.

When Sheila left to go to lunch, the Supervisor went to her station, pulled open the desk drawer and, sure enough, discovered a can of beer. The Supervisor left a note on Sheila's computer asking her to meet her in the HR Director's office when Sheila returned from lunch. When she showed up for the meeting, she did not appear to be totally coherent. The HR Director asked Sheila if she had been drinking and she replied, "Yes."

At this point, Sheila was notified she would be sent home and given time to get herself cleaned up. She was suspended for one week without pay for drinking on the job. Her instructions thereafter were for her to contact her Supervisor after the suspension was over to discuss her return to work.

After the one-week suspension, Sheila returned to the office to resume working. With all of her office access being temporarily terminated during her suspension, Sheila was forced to check-in with security for access to the office. The security office called the HR Director and notified her one of their employees was in the lobby requesting access to the work area. Security went on to inform the HR Director the employee did not have her company identification badge and she appeared to be drunk.

The HR Director contacted the Supervisor and, together, they went to the lobby to meet Sheila. They spotted the employee sitting in one of the waiting areas, covered in biscuit crumbs on her clothes, face and in her hair from her breakfast meal. They noticed her car was still running and parked in one of the handicapped spaces with the driver's door wide open.

While the Supervisor and HR Director were speaking to Sheila, the police arrived and inquired who owned the vehicle parked in the handicapped parking space with the driver's door open. The Supervisor confirmed it was Sheila's car and asked if there was a problem. The police said, "Yes." They went on to say they had been trailing that car because they had received reports of a car weaving in and out of traffic, going across lanes, and it appeared to be headed to their office building. The car fit the description and the license plate matched the 911 calls.

When the police approached Sheila, they realized she had been drinking. At this point, the employee was crying hysterically, causing people entering the building to stop and stare at the commotion in the lobby. The police arrested her and removed her from the premises. Sheila asked her Supervisor to contact her brother and have him pick up her car. The police approved the request and then hauled her off to jail.

Sheila's brother contacted the Supervisor about two days later and informed her Sheila was admitted to inpatient rehab, and would be there for the next 30 days. He insisted she was looking to get herself cleaned up and return to work. The Supervisor ran this by the HR Director, and they agreed to approve Sheila's leave, assuring her job would be held open for her. It was truly their desire to see her get herself together and return to work.

Sheila was a single mother of two school-aged children. This behavior was a shock to all who knew her. Her co-workers, as well as her Supervisor, could not understand how or why she was bringing alcohol to work and drinking in the restroom. She was known to be a non-drinker ever since she started working for the company.

When Sheila's 30-day leave was up, she showed back up in the lobby and, following standard protocol, security contacted the HR Director to inform her of the employee's arrival. The HR Director called the Supervisor and they both went downstairs to meet Sheila, excited to see her again. They were glad to see that she looked well, healthy and ready to get back to work. When Sheila resumed work, she picked up right where she left off. She was back on the calls, getting the calls resolved quickly and her hold times were just as they had been before her issues with alcohol started.

One week later, the Supervisor received a call from another employee informing her they smelled alcohol on Sheila again. They also reported Sheila did not appear steady on her feet when she returned from lunch. The Supervisor approached Sheila and asked her to come with her. They went to the HR Director's office. Needless to say, the HR Director was shocked to see them back in her office again so soon. She asked them what was going on; however, once they came in and closed the door, she immediately knew what was going on, as she could immediately smell alcohol.

When they asked Sheila what happened, she said she just felt like she needed to have a drink. Sheila went on to say, she went out to lunch and one drink turned into four. They asked her if she drove and she confirmed she had. They inquired about the location of her car and if everyone was safe on the road. She told them her car was in the parking lot and that there were no accidents, as she only drove a short distance to a local restaurant for lunch.

The HR Director explained to Sheila, based on what she had shared with them, and the fact she just returned from leave for the same reason, they would now have to terminate her employment. With her employment ending that day, her Supervisor contacted her brother and asked him to pick her up from the office because they did not want her to attempt to drive herself home. He did as asked and apologized profusely for his sister's behavior.

The last update the HR Director received about Sheila was she was back in rehab again, but this time she would be in recovery for six months in an attempt to really get herself together once and for all. Needless to say, she drank herself out of her job!

CHAPTER 3

OFFICE PARTIES & OFFICE EVENTS = HR NIGHTMARES!

O ffice parties and other corporate offsite events are truly nightmares for Human Resources professionals. These events tend to involve lots of free alcohol, resulting in wild and inappropriate behavior by staff.

Company Party #1

Case in point, there was an annual holiday party scheduled at a healthcare IT company. The receptionist was notorious for getting extremely drunk each year. The CEO asked the new HR Manager to keep an eye on her and not let her get too drunk. They also arranged to have a car take her home, just in case they lost track of how much she drank at the party. The receptionist was over 50 years old and single with no children. Her performance in the office was exceptional. She was a great receptionist and managed the office very well. Everyone loved her.

As the holiday party picked up, the new HR Manager mingled with staff and her peers, eventually losing track of the receptionist. As feared, the receptionist managed to get extremely drunk, and decided she wanted to dance on table-tops. Unfortunately, she did not have on any underwear and persisted to lift up her skirt for everyone to see underneath. The HR Manager jumped up and grabbed her off of the table while fighting to hold her skirt down at the same time. They fell to the floor, and the receptionist began to sob like a baby. She cried, yelling that she just wanted people to like her and she wanted to have fun. The HR Manager escorted her out of the party and got her into the waiting car service. She threw up a couple of times before the car took off. The HR Manager told the driver to send the cleaning bill for the interior of the car to the CEO's attention.

Company Party #2

Another office party nightmare took place with a management consulting company. The scene was a Partner meeting offsite at a hotel, which kicked off with a cocktail reception. Most of the time, the Partners would encourage the younger associates to drink. They obviously got a kick out of seeing how far the associates would go. One associate did not fail to deliver. He went into the men's room, removed all of his clothing and returned to the gathering. He then jumped on top of a dining table and began telling each Partner a piece of his mind. Initially, everyone was too drunk — or shocked — to do anything about this, but finally one Partner grabbed him off the table and wrapped his jacket around him. He continued his rant while being escorted back to his hotel room. When the meeting officially kicked off the next morning, he came and attended as if the previous night had never happened, leaving everyone wondering if they really witnessed the events the night before, or were they all imagining his performance through their drunken stupor.

One year later, he was promoted! This is truly an example of rewarding bad behavior. The newly promoted Partner would often share his story with new hires, as if it was a badge of honor. To the HR team, it showed what type of leaders the company recognized and rewarded — not a good sign, by any means! It appeared the company's motto was, "Get wasted and get promoted!"

Company Party #3

Later that year the same company, on the last night of an annual leadership summit, the Chief Operating Officer (COO) and two female Partners got so drunk, they decided it would be a good idea to stand on a table and dance and sing karaoke. The table was not strong enough to hold them while they danced and it collapsed under their weight. One of the female Partners had on 5" stilettos! They landed in a heap on the floor, legs in the air, and drinks all over the floor, laughing hysterically. Of course, associates caught the entire incident on their camera phones and started sharing their videos almost immediately. The VP of HR instructed the other HR team members in attendance to go around to each person and demand they erase their video footage. They were hopeful they caught everyone to avoid a potentially embarrassing situation for the publicly traded company.

The next day, at the wrap-up session for the off-site meeting, the COO and two female Partners arrived late.

The female Partner who was wearing the stilettos had her foot bandaged and was in a wheelchair borrowed from the hotel. She sprang her ankle in the fall off the table. The CEO came to the wrap-up session, and made lots of jokes about the prior night's events. He was there the night before, but left early and went to his room, so he did not personally witness their performance. He did, however, get to see a video another Partner sent him (proof that HR did not catch ALL of the videographers!).

This entire event made the VP of HR very uncomfortable, especially since she had junior members of her staff in attendance. She expressed to her team that this was NOT acceptable behavior, and she expected them to keep drinking to a minimum at all future company-sponsored events. She refused to have any of her team members end up on similar videos. Needless to say, there was no fallout from the behavior at this event either, which further represented what the leadership team valued in its staff.

Company Party #4

At another company outing for a law firm, an annual team meeting was organized by one of the Senior Partners at his country club, which included access to the pool and tennis courts. The HR Director feared the thought of staff being near a pool with an open bar all day, but she gritted her teeth and went along with the agenda. Her trepidations came to fruition...there was bad behavior throughout the day. Many of the young female associates wore Brazilian-cut bathing suits and tiny, barely there bikinis, sitting and drinking between the legs of male associates! T&A all over the place! Everyone was flirting and drinking heavily. The leadership team was definitely enjoying the show.

The female associates involved in the tennis activities wore the shortest tennis skirts known to man. To anyone passing by the pool or tennis court, they would not have made the connection that this was a work function. The event truly appeared to be just a group of people hanging out with friends for the day.

The next day, the HR Director met with the Senior Partner and asked for his opinion. He said he thought the meeting overall was a success and everyone had fun. He was clueless!! She expressed her opinion, asking him to reconsider the location for his next summit and stay away from pools! He told her she needed to "lighten up" if she wanted to be part of their leadership team.

Company Party #5

A different holiday party became a nightmare for the HR team at a multimedia agency. The company hosted the holiday dinner party in a beautiful venue. The staff came dressed in their best formal attire ready to party. Of course, there was an open bar all night long, including endless bottles of wine on each table. All went well until the end of the night. A female associate was found in the restroom covered in vomit reeking of alcohol. An employee located the VP of HR and informed her of the situation. She followed the employee into the restroom where the associate was incoherent and non-responsive, slouched in the corner of a restroom stall. The VP of HR bent down to check for a pulse and realized the associate had just drunk too much and was unconscious.

The VP of HR instructed one of the other employees who was in the restroom to call 911. The incoherent associate came to the party alone, and only a few people knew her personally, as she was a relatively new employee. The VP of HR also notified the CEO, and soon the ambulance arrived. The associate remained in the hospital overnight due to dehydration. She returned to work a few days later. She was embarrassed and apologized to the CEO and VP of HR. The CEO told her, "Don't worry about it. This is what parties are for, right?" The VP of HR looked at the CEO with a stare of disbelief. But this is truly the culture they perpetuated at this company. This type of behavior was never frowned upon by the leadership team, but rather rewarded! The perception was they all worked hard, so they should play hard, too. The associate did eventually resign and go work somewhere else. The office rumor was that she was not able to get past her embarrassment. The VP of HR actually commended her for resigning and moving on. However, her story was legendary and was discussed at almost every company party thereafter.

Company Party #6

One year, the CEO of an investment-research firm decided to throw a "Summer Soirée," which included an open bar at a rooftop venue in Manhattan. It was a beautiful venue and a wonderful summer evening in the city. However, beauty quickly turned into calamity!

Two hours into the event, a female associate already had too many drinks and threw up all over the venue's security guard and was becoming belligerent with the bar staff and other patrons. The venue manager could tell by her armband she was part of the corporate party, but no one seemed to know her very well. When they failed to locate someone in charge, the venue manager made the decision to send her back to the company's office address. After the taxi left, the venue's manager went back to the rooftop and had the music turned off. He asked to meet with whoever was in charge. Since the HR Director was the only HR staff member in attendance, and the last member of the leadership team still there, he was identified as the company contact. The venue's manager explained what happened with the female employee and stated they wanted to send her home in a taxi. However, she was incoherent and could not remember her address, so instead they instructed the taxi driver to take her back to their office address! The HR Director was in disbelief and stated he must have been in the restroom when all of this was happening. He immediately left to take a taxi back to their office.

When he arrived, he found the employee sitting in a fetal position on one of the benches outside the office building, where she had been dumped by the taxi driver, smelling of vomit and urine. Fortunately, the HR Director knew her name and was able to get her upstairs where he looked up her address in their employee database. He then called a car service and took her home. Luckily, her roommate was home and let them inside. He laid her on her bed and instructed her roommate to keep an eye on her. He told the roommate to call an ambulance if the employee continued to vomit. The HR Director was called "Poppa Bear" for quite awhile following that escapade.

This was just another event that became an epic tale around the office with endless jokes by staff. What a night!!

CHAPTER 4
THE CONFERENCE ROOM

The HR Director of a medium-sized law firm received a call from the owner of their office-cleaning vendor. The vendor indicated the call was regarding the cleaning of one of the executive conference rooms. The vendor went on to share with the HR Director that a female member of his cleaning crew encountered two employees having sex on the conference room table in one of the executive conference rooms. When asked if this was a singular event, the vendor informed the HR Director it actually happened several times, and has disturbed the female office cleaner so much...she has requested to clean another part of the building to avoid encountering the couple again. He provided the HR Director with a description of the couple, along with several details of the encounters. Based on the description, the HR Director immediately knew who the "couple" was — one of their Senior Partners, who was considered untouchable, and his administrative assistant. Her dilemma now was how to address this situation with senior leadership without jeopardizing HER job!

Fortunately, the vendor was willing to provide a written statement from his employee, along with some dates and times, so the HR Director would have sufficient evidence to confront both of the law firm employees. She also asked the cleaning vendor to avoid having the conference room table cleaned. This would allow her an opportunity to find physical evidence of the encounter. Her "investigation" did not take long!

On the second night of not having the conference room table cleaned, the HR Director had the physical evidence she needed, including butt prints, handprints and prints from knees and elbows. These body impressions on the conference room table aligned with the story provided by the cleaning vendor's employee, proving her initial complaint as credible. The HR Director immediately scheduled a meeting with her boss and the Managing Partner (MP). The HR Director took both of them to the conference room to show them the "evidence," and shared the written statement from the cleaning vendor's employee. The HR Director presented a proposal to the leadership team to suspend the Partner and to move his assistant to another part of the organization to support another manager.

The Partner was married with children. His assistant was a single woman who worked for him for over seven years. She received consistently high ratings on her performance reviews and was considered a high-performing (HiPo) employee. They had zero grounds to terminate her, and the MP was not supportive of terminating either of them. He declared it a mistake, and said he would handle speaking with the Senior Partner to get his side of the story. Additionally, the HR Director was instructed not to say anything to either employee until the MP gave her permission to do so, and to put the conference room back on the cleaning crew's nightly cleaning schedule.

After two weeks of private discussions, the MP shared with the HR Director and her boss that he felt any suspension of the Senior Partner was too harsh, would negatively impact their clients and would cause a lot of office gossip. His recommendation was a compromise of the HR Director's original proposal. The administrative assistant would be assigned to another Partner. Basically, they would swap administrative assistants from different departments to put some distance between the Senor Partner and his assistant. The MP instructed the Senior Partner to "keep his pants on", keep his mouth shut and not make any noise about the transfers. The Senior Partner was also instructed not to share any of this information with the administrative assistant, as they were certain she could have grounds to sue them. The HR Director instructions were to only share with the senior administrative assistant that another Partner required a more experienced assistant, and since she was one of their best assistants, it would be great for her career to make the transition.

The HR Director did not broach the real issue with the assistant; although the assistant was suspicious and initially stated she did not want to leave her current Partner. The assistant was visibly upset, and stated she felt she and her current Partner had a great working relationship and had a lot of projects they were in the middle of, which would not successfully transfer to a new administrative assistant. She put up a good fight, but the HR Director stood her ground.

The transfer was arranged the following week. The Partner pushed back on this plan as well, and was not very welcoming of the new administrative assistant. He reported that she was not a good match and did not meet his expectations. He complained to the HR Director time and time again, but she did not relent to his tantrums. She knew this was in the best interest of the organization and would help avoid a potential lawsuit. Of course there was lots of office gossip about the transfer…some valid…some not so much. The HR Director did not discuss the situation with anyone other than the MP and her boss. She expressed her concerns, stating it did not feel "right," since the only person truly impacted by this was the female administrative assistant. She believed there was no balance in how this was being handled. The MP argued it was a balanced approach because the Senior Partner experienced significant downtime due to the learning curve of the new administrative assistant, which had a direct impact on his capability to service their clients, which also impacted the company's bottom line, blah, blah, blah! This was a hair-scratching, nerve-wrecking situation for this seasoned HR Director. She was torn but proceeded as instructed by her leadership team.

The administrative assistant also complained about the new alignment, and said she felt she was being punished for something never explained to her. The HR Director held her ground with her as well, although she was certain the two of them were comparing notes. Her story had to remain consistent throughout the situation with all of the key players, including the other new Partner whom the assistant was now supporting.

About a month later, the HR Director received a "gift." The Senior Partner went to his boss (the Managing Partner), and reported that he had separated from his wife, and professed his love for his administrative assistant. He said he knew the HR Director and the leadership team were trying to protect the company, which caused him to make a life-changing decision to leave his wife and move his administrative assistant into a new apartment. He went on to let the MP know the administrative assistant had submitted her two weeks' notice, and would no longer work for the company. He announced he would marry her once his divorce was finalized. He also stated he was willing to keep the new administrative assistant since his former administrative assistant (and professed lover!) had approved the new arrangement. He even joked that the new assistant was not his "type," so the company would not have to worry about a repeat occurrence with her. Oh, how nice!

It took over a year, but the Partner held true to his word. He did marry his administrative assistant shortly after his divorce was finalized. He had to pay his wife a hefty settlement, along with child support for their children, and a huge chunk of his retirement fund. In the end, these two were in love, and showed the world — and the office staff — they wanted to be together. What started on a conference room table turned into their happily ever after. A few staff members were invited to the wedding. The HR Director did not make the guest list.

CHAPTER 5
THE TERMINATOR

There was a new Vice President of HR hired for a mid-sized rural hospital. The organization had not had a true HR leader in several years...and it showed! The VP of Legal managed HR for over two years. The new VP of HR found this was a bit odd, but he was told that this was an interim choice until they hired the right HR leader. The HR team was "green," mostly people transferred from other departments or hired locally with no formal HR experience, but the new VP of HR felt he could teach and coach them.

During his first three months, the VP of HR focused on assessing the HR infrastructure, which was in dire need of repair. For example, there were employee files over 30 years old that were not properly stored or archived. The VP of HR and the entire HR team worked over a period of several weeks to go through the files and assess what should be retained and what should be destroyed or shipped for offsite storage. Eventually, the HR infrastructure was re-established, inclusive of digitizing and automating where possible, making the team much more efficient. The VP of HR felt he was off to a great start, and making an immediate impact with the HR team, the employees and the leadership team.

One day, the Executive Director (ED) asked the VP of HR to come to his office for a quick meeting. When he walked into the office, there was a stack of employee files on the table. The ED asked him to take the files home and review them and confirm if they had sufficient grounds to fire any of the employees based on what was in their files. The VP of HR found the request peculiar, but was up to the task.

He took the files home and read through them over the course of a few days. After his assessment, he informed the ED that the information in the files was dated (i.e., older than six months), and he would not recommend firing the employees based off of what was currently in their files. From his immediate reaction, the VP of HR could tell this was NOT the news the ED wanted to hear.

These employees were immediately placed on their Managers' "watch list." Their Managers were informed to document any infractions so they could move to terminate quickly, basing their decision on more recent and relevant performance issues, versus the older documentation in their files. Within a matter of three months, the VP of HR helped orchestrate the termination of 10 people, some of whom were related to each other. He immediately became Public Enemy #1! He received hate mail and notes left on his windshield. He actually feared his car tires would be slashed or some other form of damage. The VP of HR shared his concerns with the ED, who told him to "man up"!

One day, the VP of HR was called into another meeting with the ED. There was an employee file for one of the Managers who had just received a Workers Compensation settlement of over $70k. The ED wanted to know if they had grounds to fire him since he got hurt on the job while violating a workplace safety policy. When the VP of HR asked how long ago had the accident occurred, he was told it was over two years ago. He informed the ED that it would be deemed retaliatory by any good attorney, and that they had no real grounds for termination at this point. The ED again was neither thrilled with the assessment nor satisfied, and was determined to rid the company of this Manager. From that day, the ED held a tight rein on the Manager, writing him up for every infraction, no matter how small. The Manager was eventually fired for coming into work late without calling, a violation of the company's "No Show/No Call" policy. There was nothing the VP of HR could do since it was clearly a policy-related termination. The leadership team considered this a *win*, and actually toasted their victory over a dinner on the Manager's last day. This is the same celebratory dinner where, after they drank multiple bottles of wine, the ED complimented a female staff member on the size of her breasts; and when the ED complained about the temperature in the room, he said he needed a thermostat remote that was so sensitive he could control it with his erect penis! Really?! The VP of HR began to feel this new job was definitely a big mistake.

In another incident at the same company, a managerial position became vacant. There were quite a few internal candidates. One of the viable internal candidates held a Master's degree, which was required for the position. When the hiring Manager asked HR to extend an offer to the internal candidate, he was asked to provide a copy of his degree, as he did not provide it when he was originally hired several years prior. When the VP of HR reviewed the copy of his degree, he informed the hiring Manager that the degree did not look legitimate. He told the Manager he would contact the school and also a degree-verification website to determine if the degree was legitimate. After some additional research, they found out the degree was not legitimate. The VP of HR recommended immediate termination.

However, before he could be terminated, the employee hurt his back while at work. He went out on a Workers Compensation claim, but once he was cleared to return to work, he was terminated for falsifying employment documents. He did not deny the degree was fake and left willingly.

The VP of HR found out two weeks later the terminated employee was an usher at his church. Awkward! The employee never mentioned the termination, nor did the VP of HR. Initially, the VP of HR tried to avoid him as much as possible at church, but ultimately they spoke about the situation once he told the ex-employee he was no longer employed at the company. The VP of HR resigned shortly after the employee's termination, as it appeared the leadership team wanted his sole responsibility to be termination of long-termed problem employees. This was NOT what the VP of HR signed up for. His job description described the role as being responsible for strategic HR initiatives and programs, and being a key member of the leadership team. During his first year at the hospital, the VP of HR helped orchestrate the termination of close to 20 people!

Since this was a small, rural town, finding comparable employment would not prove to be an easy task for these former employees. Over time, the culture proved to be a combination of *Peyton Place* and *Deliverance*! The VP of HR could not get out of there fast enough!

CHAPTER 6

THIS VICE PRESIDENT IS OUT TO LUNCH!

The HR Director of a financial-services firm received a phone call from someone stating she was about to release a story to a local newspaper and to the company's Board of Directors. The HR Director asked the woman to identify herself and she said she was the wife of a former employee.

At first, the HR Director did not think this had anything to do with the company...until the caller provided the name of one of their top Vice Presidents (VP). She went on to say this VP had been having an affair with her husband on company time. The caller stated the VP was leaving the office for over 3 hours, 3 times a week — Mondays, Wednesdays and Fridays. She went on to share her findings from a private investigator she hired a year ago to follow her husband once she suspected he was having an affair, and she was going to send this information to their local town newspaper. Since this was a publicly traded company, the HR Director reported this information to the CEO and their internal legal counsel.

They invited the woman to come in to meet with them at their headquarters so they could see what information she had, and then confirm the details of her story as much as possible before involving the VP and her immediate Manager.

About a week later, the wife came in for the meeting. The HR Director led the wife and her private investigator to a secluded conference room. The wife sat down and appeared to be shaken and upset. She had a stack of folders, photos and paperwork in her possession. During the course of the meeting, the company representatives found out not only was her husband a former employee of the company, but he also previously reported to the female VP in question. Her husband had resigned from the company about six months earlier but, based on the information the investigator provided, he and the VP had been having an affair while he was working for the VP for over two years.

The HR Director and General Counsel were instructed by the CEO to review and confirm the VP's attendance records. They met with her assistant and different members of her staff. They all confirmed the VP did take very long lunch breaks and, YES, they do believe it occurred three days a week or more. They confirmed she usually told them when leaving for lunch, but when she returned, she did not make a "big deal" about it. Instead, she would just pick up with her regular schedule. Her assistant also confirmed the VP had instructed her to block her calendar and not let any meetings be placed on her calendar until she returned from lunch. If anyone wanted to meet with her, she was told to say she was not available – without explanation, unless it was her boss, the Senior VP (SVP). If it was her boss, the assistant was instructed to call the VP immediately to let her know the SVP wanted to have a meeting with her. The VP would, in turn, contact the SVP directly to cover her tracks.

Somehow, she was able to keep this going for quite some time. While the male employee was working for her, they were able to keep up this affair within a reasonable time period of 1 to 1½ hours. But, when he got his new job, he was further away and, since he was not in a position of authority, he could not disappear for more than an hour for lunch. The VP would drive 40 minutes to meet with him for lunch at the same hotel every week and then make the 40-minute drive back to her office. In essence, she was gone three hours a day, three times a week for a total of nine hours for "lunch" every week.

While the HR Director, the General Counsel and the CEO continued with their own internal investigation, they asked the wife to leave a copy of her information with them so they could get back to her at the conclusion of their internal investigation. Three days later, they summoned the VP to the CEO's office. In the meantime, the wife assured them she would not report her findings to their town newspaper, and she would not turn anything over to the Board of Directors, allowing the company time to deal with this internally. She just wanted this VP "punished" for what she did, and wanted to be kept abreast of what the final decision would be. The General Counsel informed her this would ultimately be a company decision, and they were not under obligation to do so, but they assured her they would close the loop with her one way or the other.

With the information from the internal investigation, along with the paperwork provided by the wife and her private investigator, they called the VP in for a meeting. They purposefully booked the meeting on a Wednesday in the middle of what would have been her notorious "lunchtime." When the VP walked in, the General Counsel, the HR Director and the CEO greeted her. At this time they had not told her boss, the SVP, about the investigation because they wanted to gather all of the facts and confirm validity of the complaint before they informed him of what was going on.

The General Counsel kicked off the meeting and proceeded to ask the VP questions about her lunch period and her time away from the office. She initially claimed ignorance about how she was spending her lunch period. The General Counsel then let her know they had already met with her staff and her assistant. They also let her know they were aware she informed her assistant to block her calendar during the same time for three days per week.

The CEO asked her under what authority was she taking these long extended breaks throughout the week. They wanted to know what she was doing during these breaks, especially since she was utilizing the company car during her absences. The CEO emphasized he did not appreciate the fact she was basically abusing her privileges as a VP. The VP continued to try and deny everything by saying she was going to different client meetings and she was going to different branches of the company to meet with her virtual staff members. But the leadership team had already done their due diligence and confirmed this was NOT the case.

Once they introduced the information they gathered through their internal investigations, the VP broke down and began to cry. She asked, "Am I being fired for taking long lunches?" Their response was, "No. We just want to find out what you have been doing during your lunch breaks, and why are you taking these three-hour lunch breaks multiple days each week." Backed into a corner she finally admitted she was having an affair and she was trying to keep it from her husband. She said conducting her activities during the day allowed her to leave work and return from work at the same time each day so her husband would not become suspicious.

The General Counsel asked her for the name of her lover and, once the VP revealed his name, he stated her lover was once a company employee and left only six months earlier. When the General Counsel asked her exactly when the affair started, she stated it had started while the employee was still working for her. The VP was aware this was a violation, but stated their plan was for him to leave the company and get a new job. They figured this would make it easier and better for them to be together. They planned for him to move to another company because they were in love and were not prepared to stop the affair.

The CEO then introduced the information they obtained from the wife and her private investigator. They told the VP the wife was prepared to go to their local town newspaper and the Board of Directors to expose both of them.

At this point, after reviewing everything and hearing all of the information from the VP, the CEO left the conference room and contacted the SVP and asked him to join the meeting. The CEO updated the SVP on everything going on and he, of course, was surprised and shocked. He felt betrayed and realized he should have had more oversight of his team. He was somewhat embarrassed he had let this happen under his watch.

The CEO stated that would be a separate conversation but, more importantly, he wanted the SVP in the room when they moved to terminate the VP. The General Counsel, HR Director and the SVP returned to the conference room and joined the VP to proceed with the meeting. They found the VP sitting there with a greater intensity of nervousness, as she wondered how her fate would end with the company. When she saw her boss enter the room, she saw the "writing on the wall" and knew where this meeting was headed.

After everyone was settled, the SVP began to speak and informed the VP he had been brought up to speed on everything that had transpired and, as a result of everything they learned through the investigation, along with what she personally shared, she would be terminated effective immediately. The VP was instructed to leave all company equipment, including the company vehicle, cell phone and company ID card with the General Counsel. The VP asked if she could say goodbye to her team, but the HR Director advised against this. He recommended the best course of action for the VP was for her to leave the office immediately. They assured her they would gather her personal belongings and have everything packed and shipped to her.

While the VP took time to make arrangements to get home, the CEO called the Board President and informed him the VP had been terminated, effective immediately. In the midst of shareholders being unhappy with the company's stock prices dropping every quarter, this scandal was not something they wanted leaked to the press. They had to act quickly and delicately, and do what they needed to do to make sure this did not leak outside of the company.

No one really knows what happened to the VP since her departure from the company. There were some accounts she was working as a consultant, so the assumption is she did not land a new job. No one knows what ultimately happened with her relationship with the former employee either. The General Counsel did close the loop with the wife, and notified her the VP was no longer employed with the company. He did not provide the wife any details relating to the termination of the VP. The General Counsel suggested there was no need to make anything public, as the situation had been addressed internally and the Board President had been informed of the matter. The wife confirmed she would not move forward with taking her information public to the local newspaper or the Board of Directors. Case closed!

CHAPTER 7

NO ONE WANTS TO WORK FOR THEM - FIX IT HR!!

Although highly skilled and considered subject-matter experts, the following two *Horrible Bosses* were terrible "people managers." However, Human Resources had their hands tied in terms of disciplining these *Horrible Bosses*, since they were so highly regarded by the company leaders. HR constantly received instructions to find new staff and to keep these *Horrible Bosses* happy. This was a challenge at best!

Horrible Boss #1 was highly demanding of his staff and expected them to work the same hours he worked (14+ hour days!). He was a tyrant and very demeaning (i.e., yelled and screamed at staff, called people idiots, threw staplers, etc.)! Oftentimes, the employees were done with their work but were afraid to leave "early" for fear of being publicly embarrassed at the next team meeting. His staff would sometimes stay in the office past midnight, just to be on call in case he needed anything. They usually arrived back at work 7 a.m. the next day. This was not sustainable by any means. The HR team received constant complaints from his direct reports, and experienced 100% turnover (i.e., resignations) of his staff year-over-year due to burnout and hostile work environment. The HR Manager advised the leadership team they were ripe for a lawsuit and the best recourse was to avoid aligning staff directly under his leadership. The leadership team reached a compromise with the HR Manager to have his team report to another Director to place a buffer between him and the rest of his team.

Of course, *Horrible Boss #1* did not take this compromise lightly, and threatened to resign due to lack of support. The HR Manager assured him this was in the best interest for him and the company, since they were certain, sooner or later, they would encounter a lawsuit. Eventually, he relented, and settled in to the new working arrangement. He was embarrassed, but agreed to work through his peer to get the assistance he needed throughout the day. The company also assigned him an executive coach who was charged with helping him build up his people management and interpersonal skills. The coach discovered that *Horrible Boss #1* was not very happy at home, and took a lot of his aggression out in the workplace. He eventually decided to see a therapist and filed for divorce.

Over time, he became a nicer, gentler person who apologized to the remaining staff who used to report directly to him. He also apologized to the HR Manager who partnered with him and tried to help him through his revolving staff changes. Most of the staff still opted to stay away from him as much as possible, as no one believed he was "fixable," or that the new kinder, gentler person was here to stay. Eventually, he retired, but his reputation was the story urban legends were made of long after he left the company.

Horrible Boss #2 experienced 100% turnover (i.e., resignations) of administrative assistants throughout his tenure. His reputation was so bad, the HR team could no longer recruit for new administrative candidates from the local employment agency. The agency actually refused to send candidates for any of his open positions based on feedback from prior assistants. He and one of the Managers on his team would constantly have loud disputes in the office hallways, in each other's office and during team meetings in conference rooms. The HR Director felt confident *Horrible Boss #2* was on the autism spectrum with a severe case of obsessive-compulsive disorder (OCD). For example, he would demand where his assistants should place staples on documents they submitted to him, and would return documents to them with the staple circled and a Post-It© instructing them where to place the staple before returning the document to him.

Over the years, the HR Director received disturbing complaints from his former assistants, including one who indicated she had stopped menstruating due to the stress of working for him. Another male assistant placed empty bullet shell casings on his desk as a sign to *Horrible Boss #2* to stay away from him and only communicate with him through emails. And yet another assistant indicated her hair was falling out as a result of the stress she experienced from working for him. The HR Director had to act quickly, as these employees were placing the company on notice of a potential harassment or hostile work environment lawsuit - or worst - with each of their complaints!

The HR Director spent a lot of time counseling *Horrible Boss #2*, including meetings with him and his team Manager who he argued with in public settings. In these meetings, he would become emotionally overwhelmed and cry. This is the first and only instance where this HR Director experienced a grown man sobbing and totally breaking down in front of her. It was difficult to maintain her composure, but she was a seasoned Human Resources professional, and was able to stay focused. Eventually, the HR Director realized he liked to play the victim, and the tears were all part of his act to gain sympathy. He claimed to be overworked and stressed-out. He always ended the meetings stating he would do better and apologize to his team. It was always a temporary respite from his well-known behavior.

The HR Director eventually told his Supervisor if the company was not willing to terminate him, then there was little HR could do to help them. The HR Director recommended the company only hire temporary assistants for him until they made a final decision about how to handle his inappropriate workplace behavior. By the time the HR Director resigned and moved on to a new opportunity, *Horrible Boss #2* was STILL employed with the company. Human Resources professionals pick their battles every day, and sometimes this means leaving them behind and moving on!

CHAPTER 8

MANAGER IN THERAPY?

A customer-service Manager at a healthcare facility had an employee who was not performing very well. The Manager complained, but did nothing in terms of writing her up or disciplining her in any way. He would just talk about how bad her work was to anyone who would listen, including the HR Manager, who advised him repeatedly to document the performance issues.

One day, the employee did not show up for work, and was out of the office for two days without calling in or showing up for work. This was a clear violation of the company's "No Call/No Show" policy. The Manager waited until the second day before contacting his HR Business Partner about the situation. The HR Business Partner notified the HR Manager and she, in turn, met with the Manager to gain some clarity on the issue. The HR Manager asked the Manager if he tried to reach out to the employee directly, and the Manager confirmed he had not. When asked why, he said he saw this as a great opportunity to terminate the employee without having to go through the paperwork and documentation process. According to company policy, if an employee has three consecutive days of "No Call/No Show," immediate termination would be approved and classified as voluntary. The HR Manager advised against this, and insisted he give her a call. However, the Manager was adamant this was not something he wanted to do, nor did he want anyone from HR to reach out to her. He wanted to bide his time to see if she would call or show up on the third day. The HR Manager did not agree with this choice, but left the final decision up to the Manager, telling herself the role of HR is "Advisor", and not responsible for hiring or firing outside of their own departments.

On Day 3, the employee did not show up for work. About two hours after the official start of the day, the Manager appeared in the HR Manager's office. His face was as white as a sheet of paper. It was clear to the HR Manager *SOMETHING* was wrong, but she could not guess *WHAT* was wrong. Since he was such a dramatic chronic complainer, the HR Manager did not expect anything too serious. She immediately asked him what was going on. He stated he had just received a call from the employee's mother informing him the employee committed suicide in a local hotel. He went on to say the family had been looking for her for a couple of days, and actually found her through the county morgue when they submitted a missing persons report to the police. The HR Manager fell to her knees, started crying and repeatedly said, "We should have called her! I should not have listened to you!"

By this time the HR Business Partner and a few other members of the HR team ran to the HR Manager's office when they heard the commotion. They opened her door and saw the HR Manager on the floor crying and the Manager crying as well. The Manager just kept saying over and over, "I'm so sorry! I thought I was doing the right thing!"

The HR Manager pulled herself together and told the team what happened. By this time, the HR Business Partner, as well as the other HR team members, began crying as well. The HR Manager went to her boss' office and notified him the HR team would be taking the rest of the day off because of what had happened to the employee. They were ALL distraught, and would be in no position to be of good service to anyone that day. Her boss agreed and sent a companywide email out on her behalf.

The HR team was dismissed for the day and, before leaving, the HR Manager contacted the Employee Assistance Program (EAP), and asked them to have a grief counselor on-site for the remainder of the week, which they agreed to do immediately. The entire HR team then left for the day.

While the HR Manager was home, she sent an email to her boss and stated she wanted to immediately change the policy to state if an employee is out without calling in or showing up after ONE day, the manager is to notify Human Resources. Human Resources would then try to make contact with the employee or any emergency contact provided in the employee's personnel records. Her boss agreed to the change, and she implemented the revised policy and notified all of the Managers via email that afternoon.

The next day, when the HR team returned to work, the HR Manager noticed the Manager was still out. He did not actually return to the office until a week later. Upon arrival to the office, the Manager met with his boss and expressed he was to blame for the employee's suicide. He also stated he felt everyone at the company blamed him. As a result, he was now undergoing therapy because of this unfortunate occurrence. He went on to request a sabbatical to assess whether or not he should continue working for the company, because he felt every time he walked into a room, people were talking about him and judging him. He was becoming somewhat paranoid and reclusive. He began to make the situation about himself...when it really had nothing to do with him! This was a traumatic event for the entire company!

Ultimately, everything around the office settled down. The Manager took three months off as an approved sabbatical. When he returned to work, everything was, somewhat, back to normal. In the end, the HR Manager found it very interesting the Manager actually turned the situation into something about himself, versus where he failed as a Manager. He did eventually resign, as he was not able to continue to face his team and co-workers. In the end, the HR Manager and other company leaders believed this was the best decision for him and the company.

CHAPTER 9
THE RESTROOM

A small company with about 25 employees had one female restroom and one male restroom, each with only one stall. The office was very small and intimate, resulting in very little room for privacy.

There was an instance when the female employees complained to the HR/Office Manager that there was a particular female employee who would use the restroom and no one wanted to use it after her due to a pungent odor. Oftentimes, they would "hold it,"; use the men's restroom; use a public restroom on another floor; or wait until the odor faded before entering the restroom. They just refused to go to the restroom immediately after this particular employee.

Three female employees served as representation for the rest of the female staff. They approached the HR/Office Manager as a cohort to discuss their concerns. The female representatives indicated they were aware of who the restroom culprit was, and they were pretty certain it was her odor hindering them from wanting to use the female restroom. The HR/Office Manager said she would try to go into the restroom after this particular employee, as she personally had not experienced any abnormally bad odor. In the past, when she noticed there were times there was an odor, she made sure there was plenty of automatic air fresheners and can air-freshener sprays in each restroom. The female cohort expressed it was time for the issue to be addressed, as they were growing tired of "holding it" or sneaking into the men's restroom. The HR/Office Manager informed the female representatives they needed to keep this matter confidential, and not discuss it any further in the office. They assured her they would comply. In turn, the HR/Office Manager assured them she would address it in a very tactful and professional way, and hopefully get the issue resolved quickly.

Over the next few days, the HR/Office Manager kept an eye out to determine when she would enter the restroom after this particular employee. One day, the female cohort signaled to the HR/Office Manager it was a good time to check into their concern, as the employee they complained about had just exited the restroom. Upon entering the restroom, the HR/Office Manager immediately identified what the female cohort was complaining about. There was a very strong, pungent odor in the restroom following this employee's exit.

The HR/Office Manager asked to meet with the employee a couple of days later. When the employee, Melissa, came into her office, she appeared a little nervous. She had no clue why she was being summoned. Melissa was a pretty

good employee in terms of performance, and had no attendance issues, so she did not understand why she was being
called in to HR.

The HR/Office Manager began the conversation with a
few pleasantries: "How are you doing?"; "How's everything
at work?"; "How's everything at home?" She and Melissa had
a good rapport, so the HR/Office Manager felt comfortable enough to ask her such questions. Once they covered
the pleasantries, she asked Melissa if she was experiencing any health issues. Melissa looked a little puzzled, but
replied, "Not that I'm aware of. Why do you ask?" The HR
Manager explained she wanted to speak to her - *woman-
to-woman*, to let her know some of her female peers were
complaining about going to the restroom after her because
of a very strong odor. The HR/Office Manager went on to
explain she actually had the same experience the other female employees had experienced a couple days prior. Of
course Melissa was very embarrassed, but admitted she had
noticed she did have an odor, but she did not know what it
was. She assured the HR/Office Manager she would make
an appointment to see her gynecologist immediately. The
HR/Office Manager expressed her appreciation, and said
she understood how uncomfortable and embarrassing a
situation like this could be, but, as a woman, she wanted
her to be aware of this so she could take care of herself. She
extended the offer, stating if there was anything she could
do for her, just let her know.

About three days later, Melissa returned to the office
after being out on sick leave and asked to meet with the
HR/Office Manager. She began the conversation by telling
the HR/Office Manager she went to the doctor as they had

discussed earlier and, upon examination, the doctor discovered there was a tampon left inside of her. When the doctor asked her if she knew how long it had been inside her, Melissa said she was not certain, but if she had to guess... she would say probably about two months. She came to that conclusion because she recalled a night around that time when her husband wanted to have sex. She let her husband know she was still on her period, but he insisted and, with it being the middle of the night, it slipped her mind she had a tampon in. She guessed that, in the midst of a heated moment, the tampon was pushed deep inside of her. The gynecologist informed Melissa this was dangerous for her health, and it was the sole reason why she was experiencing the odor, which he also sensed upon his examination of her. The doctor went on to say she should thank the HR/Office Manager for insisting she go to the doctor to find out what was going on with her health, instead of hoping it would "fix itself."

In the end, the employee had the tampon removed and looked, and SMELLED, much better. Without going into details, The HR/Office Manager assured the female representatives everything had been taken care of and they were free to use the restroom. Her female co-workers, although somewhat hesitant about entering the restroom after her, eventually realized the issue had been resolved. From then on, there were no further complaints from the female staff about the restrooms again. The HR/Office Manager was relieved to return to her regular HR and office management duties. Problem solved!

CHAPTER 10

TERMINATION CAMPAIGN: *PART I*

There was a CEO who had a small marketing and media firm. He started the company about five years prior to hiring his first HR Manager. When the new HR Manager joined the team and had been there for about three months, the CEO met with her in regards to some changes he wanted to make on his leadership team. He had ideas, but was unsure about how to go about moving forward. He asked the HR Manager what tools or types of processes he could use to start formally assessing his senior management team. The HR Manager suggested a 360-Feedback. She explained this method would give him an opportunity to get a sense of how everyone in the company, as well as clients and vendors, viewed their professional relationships with his top people.

The CEO met with the HR Manager on a weekly basis to gain her perspective of how she thought the leaders functioned as department heads and as part of his leadership team. She did have some concerns about one or two of them and shared those concerns with him. The CEO decided to have his VP of Operations, CFO, VP of IT and two Account Management Directors go through the 360-Feedback process. The process took place after the HR Manager had been there for approximately six months, so she was still relatively new and was still getting to know the leadership team and employees. The CEO instructed the HR Manager to proceed with the 360-Feedback through a third-party vendor as part of that year's annual performance review process.

The HR Manager was placed with the task of finding a third-party company to conduct the 360-Feedback process to ensure that feedback remained impartial. After doing some research, the HR Manager was able to find a company to manage the program for the ENTIRE management team. This would help ensure the process would not isolate the few leaders the CEO really had his eye on.

Approximately two weeks later, the results from the 360-Feedback were delivered to the HR Manager. After reviewing the documentation, it was pretty clear a lot of people thought less favorably of the VP of Operations, the CFO, as well as the two Account Management Directors. This came as a bit of a surprise to the CEO, considering that these individuals had been with him almost from the start of his business. In fact, the VP of Operations was the one who really ran the company for him, and actually handled Human Resources prior to the hiring of a formal HR Manager.

After reviewing the 360-Feedback results, the CEO met with the HR Manager to go through the reports. He shared with her he wanted to use the information to offer exit packages to those who received the most irreparable and negative feedback. He wanted to start eliminating them one-by-one, and wanted to start with his VP of Operations.

Considering the overall feedback in the individual reports, the HR Manager was supportive, but felt the CEO should at least provide his direct reports some sort of leadership development first. The leadership team had not seen their reports, as the third-party administrator delivered them directly to the HR Manager. She was certain all of this would come as a surprise to them. This was the first time they would receive this type of feedback, since the CEO had never provided constructive feedback to any of them before.

Although he was nervous and uncertain of the outcome, the CEO agreed to meet with each leader individually, along with the HR Manager, to go through the feedback. Upon review of the feedback, he agreed to establish a three-month probationary period in which they had to, basically, turn everything around with their teams and clients. The HR Manager agreed with his strategy, as she felt this was a fair process considering he was giving them a chance to make things right.

He first met with the VP of Operations, who was completely taken aback by the feedback in his report. There were accusations of him being somewhat of a bully and having very poor social skills. The feedback even went into details about him smacking his mouth when he ate food! Some of the comments in the report were ridiculous. Even the clients had some derogatory things to say about him. Needless to say, he was shocked by the feedback and was hurt and deeply embarrassed. Again, this was the first time he received this type of feedback.

There he was ... sitting in front of a relatively new HR Manager and his boss, the CEO. With all of this on the table, the VP of Operations left the meeting red-faced and upset. He asked to go home early, which the CEO obliged. The following day, he actually came in and turned in his resignation.

After receiving the news of the resignation, the CEO called the HR Manager into his office and stated the resignation was actually a relief to him. Now he would not have to extend a severance package. The HR Manager thought this was an interesting way of looking at the situation, as this was someone who had been with him from the very beginning. To say the HR Manager was a bit surprised by the CEO's excitement about the resignation was an understatement. All she could think was "Hmmm...if he'll do that to him, what would he possibly do to me?"

The next meeting was with the two Account Management Directors. In each of their separate meetings, both individuals were also surprised by the feedback they received. Much of the feedback they received came from their direct reports, which discussed their brassiness and unwillingness to collaborate. The feedback even went as far as to say they were tyrants in the office, and they fed off of each other when making work decisions. One report defined them as being cliquish — if one of them disliked an associate, the other one would have an automatic dislike for the associate. The CEO and HR Manager explained to them how this type of behavior was unfavorable and could be interpreted as nepotism and bullying in the workplace. In the end, both Directors followed in the steps of the VP of Operations and decided to leave the company shortly after receiving their quarterly bonuses.

The meeting with the CFO produced the same reaction as the rest — outright surprise! When the CEO and HR Manager met with him, he was shocked by the feedback. There were a lot of statements referring to him as being impersonal, grumpy and negative. He did not see himself that way, but this was apparently a blind spot for him. Ultimately, he, too, decided to resign.

So, over a period of a year, the entire original leadership team had resigned. These are employees who had been with the CEO from the early stages of his business. However, the CEO saw their resignations as a *win*. He did not have to pay severance packages, which is what he originally planned to do three months after they received the 360-Feedback reviews.

After the last leader resigned and the dust began to settle, the CEO called the HR Manager into the office. He presented her with a bonus for her advisement on allowing the individuals to have a three-month developmental period instead of immediately firing them. He thought as a result of waiting, the HR Manager actually saved him money since he did not have to pay out large severance packages.

Of course she accepted the bonus – she was no fool! However, while she was still employed there, she was secretly planning her own exit strategy. She decided early on that she did not like his management style or the culture he was setting. She resigned shortly after her bonus check cleared!

CHAPTER 11

TERMINATION CAMPAIGN: *PART II*

The HR Director was employed with her company for approximately three years. Her manager, the Senior VP of HR, was based out of headquarters located in Australia. Within the last year of her employment, the Senior VP of HR noticed the HR function was not progressing as fast as she had hoped it would under the HR Director's leadership. The HR Director had a team of 10 people reporting to her, some who complained directly to the Senior VP about the HR Director's management style. Collectively, her staff expressed concerns regarding the HR Director being overwhelmed and unable to handle the role. After hearing this, the Senior VP had a discussion with the CEO of the local branch, and asked the CEO for his opinion of the HR Director's performance. The CEO stated he was not getting what he needed from the HR Director, but was willing to settle since the Senior VP was backing her up from headquarters in Australia. He looked at the lackluster performance as something he just had to deal with since the Senior VP could not be in the local office all of the time.

The Senior VP processed all of the feedback she received and decided that she would conduct a meeting with all of the HR Director's team members, as well as her peers. She needed to obtain a real understanding of what their opinion was of the HR Director in terms of how well she was performing in her role. This, in theory, was an informal 360-Feedback review.

Although the HR Director was aware these meetings were taking place, the explanation she received was, they were gathering information to give her some useful feedback she could use for developmental purposes, and to be able to improve the Human Resources function. The Senior VP emphasized this was important for her as well, since she was based abroad and was only able to meet with her for one-on-one feedback sessions quarterly.

The meetings were completed within a week. The Senior VP took people out to lunch, out to dinner, out for drinks, and she met with different people in their offices. At the conclusion, she circled back and met with the CEO. She and the CEO reviewed all of the notes from her meetings with everyone and, unfortunately, the feedback was not favorable.

When the Senior VP met with the HR Director, she shared the feedback, but withheld the source of each comment. The Senior VP informed the HR Director the initial purpose of the feedback process was solely intended for developmental purposes. But, after reading through the feedback, the intent had changed. The HR Director was completely shocked by what she was hearing. This was the first time she EVER heard such feedback in her entire career! She had certainly never heard it from her Senior VP or the CEO during the course of her employment with the company. After all, she was a part of the senior leadership team and was present in those meetings with the company leaders every month. Why had no one ever mentioned anything to her about their lack of confidence in her ability to lead the Human Resources function? She was devastated. That said, the HR Director no longer felt confident she could do the job. The Senior VP agreed. Based on their assessment of the feedback, she and the CEO felt the role was more than the HR Director could handle.

The Director was given a 30-day termination notice. She was asked to finish wrapping up some pertinent projects over the next month. Although she was offended by the request, she agreed to finish the tasks. She was given a robust severance package to provide her a soft landing until she found her next opportunity. On her last day of work, she left embarassed and opted out of any farewell luncheons or dinners. She just wanted to disappear and move on with her life.

CHAPTER 12
EVERYONE KNOWS
HER NAME

HR Professionals are not without their own office scandals. This is the story of a HR professional who became intertwined in her own corporate scandals.

Jennifer was a young new hire at a large banking institution. She was a very attractive young lady who moved to New York from Kentucky with her boyfriend, and wanted to immediately jump into the New York lifestyle.

The banking institution was known for hiring young people straight out of college and training them in the industry. One of the strategies this company practiced was purposely searching for "attractive" people. They felt they would have a better chance at winning high-income clients if they had attractive people on their client-engagement teams.

One of Jennifer's duties in her new Human Resources role was to go to college campuses to recruit new graduates for the firm. Jennifer became known on the Campus

Recruiting team as "*the one to send in to talk to the guys.*" She had a knack for getting young men interested in the company, and was able to bring a lot of new recruits in. Now, she did have a flirtatious way about her, but the HR Director ignored it for the most part, because she considered it harmless. Plus, everyone on the team knew she had relocated to New York with her boyfriend.

At a holiday party, a roommate of one of the recent new hires shared with Jennifer's colleague, Kirk, he was tired but could not go home that night. When Kirk inquired why he could not go home, he responded, "Don't you know? Your co-worker is sleeping with my roommate and they asked me not to come home tonight." Kirk scrambled his brain trying to figure out which HR co-worker he could possibly be talking about, since most of the members of the HR team were either married or in committed relationships. Kirk figured maybe the employee was mistaken. Maybe it was someone he *thought* was on the HR team but actually was not. Kirk really did not give much more thought about the conversation afterwards.

The next day, when everyone returned to work, Kirk saw another new hire and Jennifer exiting the subway station together and heading to the office. He stayed back so he could actually see if the two of them would enter the office together. Kirk witnessed them stopping for breakfast and noticed they seemed very cozy with each other. He then saw them enter the building together, but they separated at that point, going to different elevator banks to give the impression they were not together.

Kirk went to the HR Director and told her what he saw and what he learned at the holiday party from the new hire.

The HR Director informed Kirk there was not much that could be done about someone's personal life. Kirk insisted Jennifer's behavior was making the company look bad because she was actually the face of the company at campus recruiting events. He also wondered how they could be sure she was not sharing confidential HR matters with the employee. His primary concern was HR professionals should not be involved in relationships with employees. The HR Director agreed with his concerns, and said she would talk to Jennifer and try to do a little bit of probing. She went on to say she appreciated the fact he brought all of this to her attention first.

The HR Director met with Jennifer the next day and said she just wanted to check in to see how things were going for her. She casually asked her how things were going between her and her boyfriend since their relocation, as she knew it was a big move for them. Jennifer shared with the HR Director they were, in fact, having problems regarding his career goals. He was experiencing some difficulty transitioning into the highly competitive hedge-fund industry in New York, so he quit without having another job! Her boyfriend recently informed her he decided he would like to pursue a full-time career in acting. With him not bringing in any consistent income, and spending money on acting lessons, the financial burden fell solely on her. Jennifer began to break down a bit in front of the HR Director.

The HR Director comforted her by telling her she was certain everything would work out for the best. She quickly changed the subject and reminded Jennifer as an HR professional, it was their duty to keep a professional distance between themselves and employees. This practice was in place to prevent the appearance of one employee being favored over another, and ensured employees felt comfortable speaking with HR confidentially. Jennifer expressed her awareness of the company policy, but was curious as to why she was even bringing this up. The HR Director told Jennifer she had reason to believe she was involved in a personal relationship with one of the new recruits. The HR Director expressed her sincere apologies if the accusations were not factual. However, she did share with Jennifer she had been notified she and one the new recruits were seen in some very "comfortable" situations. For all intents and purposes, it appeared the two of them were in a personal relationship.

The HR Director stated in light of what Jennifer had shared about her relationship problems, she was beginning to wonder if there was more to it than just a friendship. Of course, Jennifer denied any inappropriate behavior with any employees. She was adamant the employee was thinking about leaving the company, and she was merely trying to convince him to stay since she was involved in his recruiting. She went on to say he was sharing with her some difficulties he was experiencing on a client engagement, and sought advice from her. She assured the HR Director there was nothing more than a platonic relationship between the two of them.

Three months later, the Human Resources team was invited by one of the company leaders to his annual team outing at his private golf club. This was a big team meeting consisting of approximately 80 people. It was the HR team's first time ever being invited to be a part in the annual event. Jennifer showed up and, instead of coming dressed in golf attire, she came adorned in tennis attire — a VERY short tennis skirt outfit!

The HR Director was taken aback by her appearance, so she pulled Jennifer aside and asked her if she thought her outfit was appropriate for the occasion. Jennifer's reasoning was she regularly plays tennis, so she wore what she felt was appropriate for the activities she planned to participate in that day. The HR Director explained, since golf was the occasion and the rest of the HR team was dressed in golf attire, it seemed obvious she, too, should follow suit. She reminded Jennifer all attendees had received the recommended dress code from the golf club. The HR Director was concerned with this being their first time attending the event, her appearance would ruin their chances of receiving future invitations. Jennifer said she had an outfit for dinner and she was more than willing to change into that outfit if it would make her feel better. The HR Director's response was, "Yes. Please do!"

When Jennifer walked away, one of the company leaders approached the HR Director and said he needed to speak with her concerning Jennifer. The first thing he brought to her attention was Jennifer's attire, which the HR Director quickly assured him she had already addressed and it had been taken care of. The next thing the business leader shared was that he had heard rumors about Jennifer from quite a few of his associates. Apparently, Jennifer had been in affairs with at least two of the new associates, and her name was not very well-respected among the new recruits. He also shared there was a running wager to see who she would end up leaving this particular event with by the end of the night. The HR Director was surprised by his comments, and stated while she appreciated him bringing this to her attention, there was little she could do about what someone did in his or her personal life. The business leader advised she may just want to be aware of Jennifer's reputation and its impact on the HR team. The other members of the HR team were viewed as professionals, but her team was becoming the butt of many jokes thanks to Jennifer's rumored behavior. People were beginning to wonder if there were other people on the team behaving like Jennifer. The HR Director assured him she would take care of this and have it handled.

When they returned to the office the next day, the HR Director met with Jennifer. Upon arriving at her office, Jennifer was exacerbated and looked at the HR Director as if to say "What now?" The HR Director ignored Jennifer's attitude and informed her what had been shared by the business leader, as well as what she had personally witnessed regarding her flirtatious behavior at the event the night before. The HR Director told Jennifer she observed her consuming quite a few drinks. The more she consumed, the more relaxed and flirtatious she became. She also expressed she was concerned about the impact of Jennifer's behavior on the reputation of the HR team. When Jennifer heard all of this, she began to admit to the HR Director she might have a problem. When the HR Director inquired what she thought her problem was, Jennifer revealed she believed she might be a sex addict. The HR Director did not really know how to respond to her admission, so she asked Jennifer whether or not she would feel comfortable seeking counsel for her issue through the Employee Assistance Program (EAP). Jennifer agreed to give it a try, considering she was still having problems with her boyfriend and she was no longer attracted to him. The aggravation she was experiencing from her relationship was causing her to get relief by having affairs with multiple men…and a few women. Although Jennifer agreed to counseling, the HR Director had to make it a mandate she follow through on this, but confirmed her confidentiality would be protected by the EAP team.

After another week, the HR Director had no indication Jennifer reached out to EAP. She became frustrated with all of this, so she decided to call Jennifer back into her office for a follow up discussion. The HR Director explained to Jennifer she could not take a chance with someone so new to the team behaving so badly, especially to the point where business leaders were discussing her behavior and personal life. The HR Director informed Jennifer she would have to suspend her and, hopefully, during this time, she would reach out to EAP to get the help she needed. Jennifer told her she did not need any help, and there was no need to suspend her because she was resigning effective immediately!

When the rest of the team learned of Jennifer's resignation, they held a mini-celebration. They were relieved she was no longer a part of the HR team, as she was ruining their reputation they fought so hard to gain. Although the HR Director informed her team their celebratory behavior was not appropriate, she was secretly relieved as well.

CHAPTER 13
REALLY SHORT STORIES

She Wore WHAT?

There was a supply company with a Customer Service Representative position open for a while. They had interviewed a few candidates and had not really found anyone they liked. They posted the job again and received some new candidates who they were interested in interviewing. The Recruiter and Hiring Manager were both men. However, most of the applicants consisted of females, likely due to the nature of the role.

It was the day of the in-person interviews for candidates who had been selected by phone and resumé interviews. There were approximately 6 candidates scheduled for the day. Interviews ran anywhere from 30-45 minutes. In between interviews, the Recruiter noticed a young lady sitting in the lobby. The receptionist informed him the young lady was there to interview for the Customer Service

Representative position. The Recruiter greeted her, but was quite surprised by her appearance.

Here is what she had on: full-faced makeup (including false eyelashes, very bright red lipstick, and dark, smoky eye shadow); a very short and tight dress with lots of cleavage and leg showing; 6-inch platform heels; and a sequined evening clutch in her lap.

The Recruiter assumed this was a mistake, and perhaps she was actually at the wrong company. She confirmed the name of the person who scheduled her for the interview that day. He then acknowledged he was, in fact, the interviewer who confirmed her appointment. When she gave him her name, he confirmed she was, indeed, on the schedule to be interviewed that day.

Since she was there to be interviewed, he did not want to be rude and turn her away just because of her appearance, so he invited her into his office for the interview. When she came in, the Recruiter asked the Hiring Manager to join them because he did not want to be alone with her. She was very attractive, and he did not want there to be any appearance of anything inappropriate taking place during her interview.

The Hiring Manager was also shocked by her appearance, and did not really know how to take the candidate seriously. Neither the Recruiter nor the Hiring Manager could stop focusing on her appearance — mainly, her cleavage and legs. Throughout the interview, they tried to be as serious as they could. In the end, once the candidate felt the interview was coming to a close, she said she wanted to thank them for seeing her. She also stated they should know that she does not always dress like this for interviews, or to come to work. She let them know she had been out at a club the night before and had been drinking and did not want to take the chance of going home and falling sleep, and possibly miss her interview. She went on to say she stayed up all night and, because she had not gone home yet, she did not have a change of clothes, and basically came straight from the club for her interview. She said she left the club at 6 a.m., went for breakfast, and then had her date drop her off for her 8am Monday morning interview.

Following her initial phone screen, the candidate was one of the people who they thought would be a good fit for the position, because she had really good customer-service experience and a great phone personality. Even in person, she came across as someone they thought could do the job well but, of course, they had to get pass her club appearance.

Once she gave a logical explanation for her attire, they were more at ease and felt confident this appearance was something they would NOT see at work if they hired her. They told her what the dress code was for the company, and she assured them she knew how to dress appropriately, as the company she worked for before had a business-casual dress code. She really hoped they would consider her for the job, despite the fact she was a little hung over and still dressed from the night before. She hoped her honesty and transparency would give her an edge over the other candidates.

After she shook their hands and left the building, everyone in the office began laughing and talking about her. They could not believe someone would come dressed like that for an interview. Everyone kept saying, "She wore *what* to the interview?!" This became an inside joke whenever a candidate arrived at the company dressed in weird attire for an interview.

In the end, they DID hire her and she actually performed very well. After two years in the Customer Service role, she was promoted. The hiring team was glad they gave her a fair chance and saw past her wardrobe and outside appearance during her interview.

Voodoo Priestess

This story takes place at a unionized nursing home. Among the nursing staff, there was one nurse in particular, Maria, who had attendance and performance issues. Due to the fact Maria was in a unionized position, any type of disciplinary action had to be orchestrated through her union representative — much to the HR Director's chagrin. Maria received a final warning regarding her attendance, and was told the next time she came in late, or had any type of performance issues, they would move to terminate her.

To say the least, Maria was a *unique* person. She had a collection of dolls — male and female — on her desk, made of cloth and were adorned with yarn for hair. They each looked homemade. She also had several pieces of artwork on her desk that appeared to be religious artifacts. There were people in the office that complained to the Supervisor about the fact Maria would mumble during the day and did weird rituals with the dolls. They suspected she was practicing some sort of voodoo at her desk. The Supervisor took this as a joke and simply laughed it off.

One day Maria was almost an hour late, and did not call to notify her Supervisor that she was running late. When she arrived, the Supervisor was waiting for her and imme-diately asked her to meet him in the HR Director's office. When she came in, Maria asked if she could have her Union Representative present, which the Supervisor welcomed. The Union Rep was on site, so she was able to have him come to the meeting with the HR Director and her Supervisor. When everyone was settled in the office, the Supervisor stat-ed today was the fifth time Maria arrived late for work, and she had already been issued a final warning. She had also been counseled, and even suspended at one point, for atten-dance and punctuality issues. Even after all of the corrective behavior actions, Maria still continued to arrive at work on her own schedule. The Supervisor went on to say, since they were at the point of the final warning, they wanted to pro-ceed with terminating her effective immediately.

Maria immediately sat on the floor, crossed her legs and began chanting. No one in the room could figure out exactly what she was doing. The Supervisor tapped her on the shoulder and asked her if she could please return to her seat, but she did not respond. Her eyes were rolling up into the back of her head. They could only see the whites of her eyes. She continued to mumble and chant, ignoring attempts from the Union Rep and others to get her atten-tion. They called Maria by name and informed her today was her last day because they were terminating her. Upon hearing this, she jumped to her feet and, in one fell swoop, she turned to them and said, "You do not know my powers! I'm a voodoo priestess and I've cast a spell on all of you!"

She threatened them with erectile dysfunction and in-fertility, because they did not respect her powers. She also stated she needed to go to her desk to retrieve her "dolls".

The HR Director and Union Rep felt Maria's behavior and outbursts were very bizarre, and viewed her as being "nuts." They did not think twice about her threats. The Union Rep escorted Maria to her desk and allowed her to collect all of her items. When he looked at the dolls, he realized they did resemble certain people in the office. He actually saw one that resembled him! The more he looked, the more he was able to identify staff members who her homemade dolls represented. There was one for the HR Director, and the nurse who sat in the cubicle next to her who she had problems with in the past. He did not recognize the others, but was sure they were for people who she worked with or was acquainted with in some way, perhaps even some of their patients. The Union Rep also paid attention to the relics on Maria's desk, and reported to the HR Director they did look as if they may be related to some sort of black magic!

In the end, they were glad she left quietly, but the whole production of her sitting on the floor with her eyes rolling up into the back of her head did spook them a little bit. The Union Rep and HR Director both agreed they did not believe in black magic, so they just chalked it up to Maria not being well mentally. However, it was quite dramatic — and comical — nonetheless! Reportedly, neither one of them suffered erectile dysfunction or infertility, and Maria's *priestess* performance became a story passed down throughout the years among the staff at the facility.